LEWIS CARROLL

LEWIS CARROLL

BY

WALTER DE LA MARE, *1873-1956*

LONDON
FABER & FABER LIMITED
24 RUSSELL SQUARE

FIRST PUBLISHED IN MCMXXXII
BY FABER AND FABER LIMITED
24 RUSSELL SQUARE LONDON W.C.I
PRINTED IN GREAT BRITAIN BY
R. MACLEHOSE AND COMPANY LIMITED
THE UNIVERSITY PRESS GLASGOW
ALL RIGHTS RESERVED

LEWIS CARROLL

E VERY CENTURY, INDEED EVERY DE-
cade of it, flaunts its own little extrava-
gancies and aberrations from a reasonable
human standard. Passing fashions in dress and
furniture, in plays, music and pictures, and even in
ideas and sentiments, resemble not only the ca-
prices of our island climate, but also the extremes
made manifest in English character, both of which
in spite of such excesses yet remain true to a
more or less happy medium. And so too with
literature.

The Victorian age was rich in these exotics. It
amuses us moderns, having dried and discoloured
them, to make little herbariums of them. We forget to remind ourselves that many of our own
prized blossoms are also of the hot-house, and
will suffer a similar desiccation. But there is one
Victorian wild flower which makes any such con-
descension absurd—and it is called Nonsense.

7

Unlike other 'sports' of its time, this laughing heartsease, this indefinable 'cross' between humour, phantasy and a sweet unreasonableness, has proved to be of a hardy habit and is still living and fragrant. And we discover it suddenly in full bloom under the very noses of Martin Tupper and of Samuel Smiles!

None even of its kindliest apologists would deny that in the earlier years of the nineteenth century the attitude of mind towards children tended to the over-solemn—a state which resembles a lantern without any light in it. Excesses may secrete their own antidotes. The mothers and fathers who had been brought up on Scotch oats with a pinch of salt for savour were to realize that honey is also a provision of nature. Yet writers who had the nursery in view, and even long after William Blake had sung of innocence, remained for the most part convinced that what is good for the young *must* be unpleasant. Their rhymes like their prose were 'nearly always in a moral, minor or miserable key'. They prescribed not simples, syrups and cordials, but brimstone. And even the treacle that accompanied it was spelt *theriaca*, and was connected with vipers. A reaction, it is clear, was bound to follow, and that reaction has perhaps reached its extreme in a good deal of the nursery literature of our own day, which is as silly, if not worse, as theirs was dismal.

Not that all the books intended for children in the early nineteenth century were concerned solely with the cautionary and the edifying, which as Charles Lamb said only 'starved their little hearts and stuffed their little heads'. And while moralisms like, ' "My dear child," answered her father, "an ox is not in the world for nothing" '; like, 'Oh, dear Mamma, if I had done as you bade me I should not have had all this pain!'; like,

> . . . When up the ladder I would go,
> (How wrong it was I now well know)
> Who cried, but held it fast below?
>> MY SISTER.

> Once too I threw my top too far,
> It touch'd thy cheek, and left a scar:
> Who tried to hide it from Mamma?
>> MY SISTER . . . ;

and

> . . . Papa, who in the parlour heard
> Her make the noise and rout,
> That instant went to Caroline,
> To whip her, there's no doubt;

—while moralisms and menaces of this order, with an occasional reminder that God's anger has no respect for persons, and far, far less for little persons, and such wolflets in lamb's clothing as *Useful Lessons*

9

for Little Misses and Masters and *Paul Pennylove's Poetical Paraphrase of the Pence Table* were prevalent, we
must not forget the many merry heart-free excep-
tions like Dame Wiggins of Lee which was the joy
of John Ruskin, or the benefactions of Dame Partlet:

> . . . That cold a fever soon brought on,
> The fever brought on death,
> So, after having made her will,
> She yielded up her breath.
>
> Yet stop your grief, for she has left
> Each little girl and b'y
> Who gets by heart this little hymn
> A cheesecake and a pie.

'The interesting and amusing moreover were then
supplanting the improving.' Many of the chap-
books for children (even of the severe order) were
illustrated with admirable cuts by artists almost as
gifted as Bewick himself, and that can hardly be
said of some of our own nursery pictorialisms.
And the pattern of versicle of the Dickory-dock
order—called a Limerick because it is said to have
emanated from Ireland—was already familiar to
young ears even in the eighteen-twenties:

> There liv'd an Old Woman at Lynn
> Whose nose very near touch'd her chin,
> You may easy suppose
> She had plenty of Beaux,
> This charming Old Woman of Lynn.

That—both in form and content—is at least to-wards Nonsense bound.

But even M. Emile Cammaerts in his *Poetry of Nonsense*—a little book as rich in appreciation and interest as it is original in theme—has been able to cite very few specimens of true Nonsense of a date prior to the nineteenth century. And the practice of the art seems to be as clearly localized in space as it is in time. The French word *non-sens* has not this particular nuance; and the German *Un-sinn* is in meaning, I gather, to madness nearer allied.

In fact M. Cammaerts has not only declared that Nonsense is wholly English in origin—'I have tried in vain to discover anything similar in French or German literature'—but he is also convinced (and seemingly with satisfaction) that it would have received a very cold welcome if it had made its appearance abroad. Only a poet could have written M. Cammaerts' book; and since he has, as it were, crossed the sea to discover this precious little autochthon, his tribute to it, as 'one of the most valuable contributions to the development and happiness of mankind', may condone a natural family pride in it and incite us to appreciate it as we should.

Whatever its origin, no little tiny boy of any time or clime who was ever dandled to the strains of *Old Mother Hubbard*, *Hey, diddle, diddle* or *Three Blind Mice*, or listened at his mother's knee to such ancient tales as *The Three Sillies*, *Teeny Tiny* and *Mr Vinegar* can have been positively untouched by its influence. Its full 'showery, flowery, bowery' summer, however, continued from the 'forties into the 'seventies. With Kate Greenaway, it hid its face in a poke-bonnet; though such recent literary lucky-bags for the nursery as *The Adventures of Dr Dolittle*, *The Pirate Twins*, *Mr Tootleoo* and *Millions of Cats* are proof that it still flourishes.

Its acknowledged masters were two in number. Two years after the appearance in 1810 of Jane Taylor's *Hymns for Infant Minds* Edward Lear came into the world. He was followed twenty years later, and two years before the death of Charles Lamb, by Charles Lutwidge Dodgson, who having latinized his Charles and transmogrified his Lutwidge, was destined at last to be known (and beloved) all the world over by his pen-name Lewis Carroll.

Lear's first *Book of Nonsense* was published in 1846, a year after the death not only of the author of *The Ingoldsby Legends* but also of Thomas Hood, a poet who because, perhaps, he was also a punster, has not even yet had his due. *The Rose and the*

Ring followed in 1855. Hood, like Lear and Thackeray, could fit pictures to his rhymes as amusing as themselves, but Lear was an artist by profession. He contributed the handsome plates to one of the earliest of the lavishly illustrated English books about birds; and it is as appropriate that its title should have so alluring a flavour as *The Family of the Psittacidae* as that the first published pamphlet in which Dodgson collaborated with his *alter ego* should have been called *The New Method of Evaluation as Applied to II.*

Lear left this world—much the poorer by his absence—in 1888, four years after Calverley. Lewis Carroll, the veritable pied piper, having visited 'valleys wild' on his way from Hamelin, vanished from its ken a little later, while Dodgson himself lived on until a year after Queen Victoria's Second Jubilee.

The rich sheaves of pure Nonsense had by then been garnered. While *The Hunting of the Snark* was of 1876 and Prince Uggug had edged into being at Hatfield to amuse Princess Alice in 1872, by 1889, when *Sylvie and Bruno* was published, another order of nonsense was in flower. *The Green Carnation* and *The Yellow Book*, are symptomatic of a very different and a wholly adult species. All satire and most parody in themselves are mortal enemies of true

Nonsense, which is concerned with the joys of a new world, not with the follies and excesses of an old. And though such sallies as 'On an occasion of this kind it becomes more than a moral duty to speak one's mind. It becomes a pleasure'; or 'A little sincerity is a dangerous thing, and a great deal of it is absolutely fatal'; or 'Punctuality is the thief of time'—though pleasantries of this nature —'truths standing on their heads to attract attention'—may faintly echo (and may even have been inspired by) Humpty Dumpty, Oscar Wilde would not perhaps have eagerly acknowledged his fat friend's genial influences; and Humpty Dumpty, quite apart from his setting, conversed in a far less worldly English.

As compared with wit, too, Nonsense, in M. Cammaerts' metaphor, is what bubble is to needle, though wit itself is powerless to prick the bubble. Twinkling on in its intense inane, it is as far out of the reach of the ultracommonsensical, the immitigably adult and the really superior as are the morning stars. That flat complacent veto—'This is nonsense!' (in the cast-iron sense of the word), while intended as a sentence of death, means little more than, '*We* are not amused.'

But what *is* this Nonsense? How does it differ from the merry, the comical, the frivolous, the absurd, the grotesque and mere balderdash? Take the Limerick. There are two distinct orders of them: the mere Limerick and the Lear Limerick. They differ far more than mushrooms from moonshine. Mere Limericks, ingenious, harmless, orthodox, may be scribbled with an effort at the rate of about two a minute. Funny, and even witty, Limericks are fairly common. A genuine Lear Limerick—and that only derivative—is unlikely to be the reward of a precious moment more than once or twice in a lifetime!

> There was an Old Man of the West,
> Who wore a pale plum-coloured vest;
>   When they said, 'Does it fit?'
>   He replied, 'Not a bit!'
> That uneasy Old Man of the West.

Again:

> There was an Old Man in a boat,
> Who said, 'I'm afloat! I'm afloat!'
>   When they said, 'No! you ain't!'
>   He was ready to faint,
> That unhappy Old Man in a boat.

Now the most apparent thing about these old gentlemen is that they are not merely respectable, they are irreproachable. Are they irrational? Surely not. *Any* old man who in questions of pure matter-of-fact declines to heed the emphatic *No! you ain'ts!* of his fellow creatures is, to say the least of it, in-discreet. And what irrationality is there in being uneasy in vests that fit not a bit, or in having the candour to confess that they don't? As for the crisis in either rhyme, it is little short of Aristotel-ian: a (seemingly) just soul endures an unde-served stroke of adversity. And could fewer words more vividly present that unhappy Old Man in a boat, whose rapture in a situation so ordinary is followed by physical symptoms so extreme after a surrender to public opinion so meek and so mag-nanimous? And last, where *is* this Old Man? In a region and a state of being solely his own, and in an Everlasting Now. Is not 'pure poetry' itself in a similar relation to actuality?

While, then, there is in these rhymes a sort of vacuum—a beauteous and balmy inanity—where the 'sense' should be—and the mere alteration of 'pale' into *new* in the first of them will show how delicate the literary poise is—there is an abun-dance of meaning. And what we call their Non-sense is nothing purely negative but lies in some celestially happy medium between what is sense and what is not *sense*. This being so, are not these two old gentlemen and their peculiarly nebulous 'they'—louring like thunderclouds on the spring-like scene—triumphantly, and up to their eyes *in*

that medium? And *'well* in?' In what then does it
consist?[1]

> They hunted till darkness came on, but they found
> Not a button, or feather, or mark,

[1]This is merely of course to skirt the fringe of the subject;
Lear sometimes lost on his rhymes what he made on his
pictures, and if pure Nonsense be the test, one concomitant
of which is that—so swiftly that we cannot possibly per-
ceive the *process*—it shall instantly, and without the least
sacrifice of its cerulean gravity, secure the hospitality of our
sense of humour, his shafts are not always on the mark.
Opinions must differ, but the Old Man with a nose, the Old
Man with a beard, the Old Man with a gong and the Old
Man in a tree perhaps fall a little short of it. The Young
Lady of Wales, the Old Lady of Chertsey, the Old Person
of Ems and the Old Man who said, 'Hush!' are exemplary;
while *Rheims* and *Wrekin* and even the *Pobble* and *The
Courtship of the Yonghy-Bonghy Bô* may leave one debating.
Of Lear's actual invention, his 'They' is perhaps his
greatest triumph—their unanimity, their cogency, their
scorn. On the technical side, as with the Petrarchan and the
Shakespearian sonnet-form, we may make our choice between the two kinds of Limerick; and there are heretics who
find the last line of the Lear kind timid, disappointing and
insipid, who prefer wit in its place—even cleverness! But
what then of that Flaubertian 'uneasy'? Indeed, as with Mr.
Belloc's Lion and its compeers (apart from its perfect
pun)—

> The Lion is the beast to fight,
> He leaps along the plain,
> And if you run with all your might
> He runs with all his mane. . . .

By which they could tell that they stood on the ground
Where the Baker had met with the Snark.

That unfortunately is the position. None the less
a glance at *Alice in Wonderland*—with its bright full

---

style, in his own particular literary nook, is Lear's open
secret. His mind was 'concrete and fastidious'; and style
with little Nonsense in it is the charm of his *Alphabet*,
with its

> O. was an Owl,
> Who continued to howl
> A monotonous song
> All the night long . . .

and its

> Q. was a Quail
> With a very short tail,
> Who fed upon corn
> Ever since he was born.
> Q!—
> Queer little Quail!

which depends for its metrical effect on a *prolonged* 'Q', perhaps educational in intention.

If, on the other hand, the last line of the Lear Limerick
fails, it fails badly. Here for example is one of the 365
rhymes from a Kate Greenaway *Birth-Book for Children*:

> There was an old person who feared
> The sun setting light to his beard;
> So he said, I will see, and sit under a tree
> Till the sun is too low to be feared.

The onset is promising, the *so* dangerous, but the dupli-
cated 'feared' is as flat as flat can be.

moon of Nonsense for lantern, may help to enlighten it a little. And first, Lewis Carroll.

Of what in the deeps of our sub-consciousness we owe to our ancestors only the confidants of Unkulunkulu can be completely aware. We know, however, that Charles Dodgson's father was renowned for his wit and humour. He delighted in any amusing joke or anecdote provided its text was not in the Bible. His father, a Captain in the 4th Dragoon Guards, was shot in the dark by an Irish rebel from the window of his cottage as he came on alone and unguarded to the appointed meeting-place where the Irishman had promised to give himself up. *That* gallant gesture is neither humorous nor nonsensical, but there is a touch of the sublime in it that is part and parcel of both.

Dodgson's great-grandfather not only loved a joke but like his great-grandson was a character. It was very cold in the winter in the vestibule, a 'low stable', as he described it, of the castle which in 1762 he was compelled to use as a temporary parsonage:

'Above it', he wrote to a friend, 'is the kitchen, in which are two little beds joining to each other. The curate and his wife lay [lie] in one, and Margery the maid in the other. I lay in the parlour *between* two beds to keep me from being frozen to death, for as we keep open house the winds enter from every quarter, and are apt to sweep into bed to me.' He was, that is, without question *the* old man in a bed.

Again:

'As washing is very cheap, I wear *two* shirts at a time, and, for want of a wardrobe, I hang my great coat upon my own back, and generally keep on my boots in imitation of my namesake of Sweden.'

A mind capable of this hospitality to life—and I am quoting from Mr. Collingwood's *Life and Letters of Lewis Carroll*—had ample room in it for a window overlooking Nonsense Lane. But whatever Charles Dodgson owed to heredity, he himself, as a small boy, was exactly the *kind* of small boy we should have expected Lewis Carroll to have chosen to grow up from. He was born in a little village called Daresbury, seven miles from Warrington. So peaceful was his father's vicarage that even the creaking of a passing farm-cart was something of an event. Here Charles spent his first eleven years. He made pets of toads and snails. He carried out little martial experiments on earthworms. He peeled rushes in the belief that the pith might be of use to the poor, though he never explained precisely how (Before he was in his teens he expressed an interest in the *looks* of logarithms, and at twelve was skilled in the invention of games. Mantled in wig and robe, and wand in hand, he practised as a parlour conjuror. He made a toy theatre and marionettes, and wrote their plays himself. And from his preparatory school in 1844 we have tidings of his first 'little girl'. 'The boys that I think that I like the best are Harry Austin and all the Tates of which there are 7 besides a little girl who came down to dinner the first day, but not since.'

His first schoolmaster reported that Charles had become skilled in Latin verse, had a 'very uncommon share of genius' and showed a 'love of precise argument'. He warned his father however against letting his son realize his superiority over his fellows. 'The love of excellence', he remarked, 'is far beyond the love of excelling'. That Charles *did* occasionally realize his superiority over his fellows, and that he even thought it desirable at times to be candid concerning the dear (or at any rate, concerning the near), is revealed by a remark he made in a letter about a relative who was for some time a resident in the Island of Tristan da Cunha. He said that he was well-intentioned but vulgar. Three months afterwards he changed his opinion. He said, 'He is now less well-intentioned and more vulgar.'

Long before he went up to Rugby in 1846—and eleven years after he had left his schooldays behind him he confessed that 'no earthly consideration' would induce him to go through them again —he set up as editor (and chief contributor) of one or two of those home-made magazines which are apt to be ephemeral but none the less give excellent opportunity and practice to the budding author. And in the shade of *The Rectory Umbrella* of 1849 appeared not only his first nonsense rhymes but his first humorous drawings. They explore a world of the grotesque already his own and are markedly in the manner of the pictures he afterwards made for *Alice in Wonderland*, and shared with Tenniel. And never surely—though in certain respects Dodgson was, it seems, a somewhat exacting collaborator—never surely were author and artist in a closer and happier partnership.

So punctilious, too, was Carroll in the choice of a frontispiece for *Through the Looking-Glass* that he consulted 'about thirty of his married lady friends before finally deciding to bestow this honour on the White Knight'. As for his early rhymes:

Fair stands the ancient Rectory,
The Rectory of Croft,
The sun shines bright upon it,
The breezes whisper soft.

22

From all the house and garden
Its inhabitants come forth,
And muster in the road without,
And pace in twos and threes about,
The children of the North.

It is the unspecified *looks* of these inhabitants,
quite apart from the dulcet air they breathe (or the
staircased family pews and preacher's hourglass
they shared in their parish church), that show how
many miles Carroll had already ventured as a boy
over the border-line of his Wonderland. The first
four lines of *Jabberwocky* too, which were afterwards expanded to twenty-eight at an evening
party, first appeared in the *Umbrella* with the title
'Stanza of Anglo-Saxon Poetry' and with a full
glossary of its terms.

Seldom has any child shown himself so clearly
the father-to-be of the man. This roving ingen-
uity, this skill in the use of words, this delight in
logic and mathematics, this passion for invention,
this penchant for puns, puzzles, parodies and pal-
aver—such things as these were to occupy Dodgson's long working days and his absorbed leisure
during the forty-seven years, from 1851 onwards,
which he spent at Christ Church. He positively
'belonged to "the house" ', says Mr. Dodgson
Collingwood, his biographer, 'never leaving it for

any length of time' from the day when on Pusey's Nomination he won his studentship there until his death. He 'became almost a part of it', the conditions of this initial privilege being celibacy and the taking of Holy Orders. He was ordained deacon in 1861, but 'never proceeded to priest's orders', says Mr. Collingwood, 'partly, I think, because he felt that if he were to do so it would be his duty to undertake regular parochial work.' 'He was essentially a religious man in the best sense of the term.'

In spite of a little impediment in speech which he shared with Charles Lamb and which added a flavour all their own to *his* witticisms also, he sometimes preached, and always anxiously prepared for these occasions. But, 'it is not', he wrote to a friend, 'good to be told (and I never wish to be told), "Your sermon was so *beautiful*."' His one object in preaching was that of 'serving God'. 'His generosity was boundless.' He never failed in patience when folly and error came to him for counsel, nor in acts of kindness.

He had pronounced views, and expressed them vigorously. And he was a precisian. If any one even of his little girls slipped in her grammar when writing to him he corrected it in his reply. Though he was wine-taster to his College, and kept a record of all the *menus* of all his little private dinner-parties, he was far from being an epicure, at any rate in food for the body. His usual lunch consisted of a biscuit or two and a glass of sherry; but he tolerated less stringent habits in others, and especially in his small guests. And when one day at one o'clock he found himself at a newly made friend's house, though he refused to eat anything, he gallantly offered to carve the mutton. But it was a joint strange to him and he made a hash of it.

His views on reviewers were also inclined to be abstemious. He assured them in one of his prefaces, first, that no doubt their remarks on his last book had been of service to it, and next, that he had refrained from reading them, since their good opinions might only have made him vain, and their chidings would have dejected him. There were occasions, however, when he risked dejecting others. For when any biblical or dubious joke was uttered in his presence on the stage, he was not content, as are most sensitive souls, to blush unseen; he rose to his feet and stalked out of the theatre. Playgoers nowadays would enjoy exceedingly active evenings in the theatre if they followed his example.

Though he was the acknowledged wit of the Common Room at Christ Church when the elect were entertained, he was naturally shy and retir-

ing. By no means a bear in company, he hated being lionized and detested publicity—a term which
it is surprising though hardly reassuring to learn
was 'in common use' as far back as 1837. He usually declined to welcome any tribute to Lewis Carroll. If his morning postman brought messages of
joy and gratitude in a strange handwriting to the
explorer of *Wonderland*, Dodgson retorted with a
punctiliously truthful, printed, and rather frigid
reply: 'Mr. C. L. Dodgson . . . neither claims nor
acknowledges any connection with any pseudo-
nym or with any book not published under his
own name.' He suggested that his pseudonymous
works should be sequestrated under the letter C in
the catalogue of the Bodleian library; and when
one afternoon at tea a genial Dean at a friend's
house referred with buoyant approval to the author of the *Alices*, he was so much vexed by this
intrusion that he implored his hostess to give him
warning when next the Dean threatened, in order
that he might retreat to his bedroom in good time.
This attitude may seem a little austere in an age
so intent as our own on all matters relating to
whom's whom—but Dodgson was of opinion,
perhaps, that though a book is public property, its
author is not; and that books best speak for themselves.

Mr. Collingwood suggests that some shadow of disappointment hung over his life; and certainly the face that is looking away from the observer in one of the best known of his photographs has a shade of the disastrous in its aspect; and even in one taken when he was twenty-three there is a tinge of melancholy. Like Edward Lear, like most jesters, he had his hours of depression; and it may be to this natural reserve that a tribute to his memory in *Punch* referred:

> The heart you wore beneath your pedant's cloak
> Only to children's hearts you gave away. . . .

One is conscious, too, of a certain primness, a slight stiffness in his later letters; and his prefaces to *Sylvie and Bruno* are oddly deficient in the good humour that may make a man tolerable company to himself even when he has a pen in his hand. In these Dodgson himself, 'tall and dark', is at times Victorian and solemn. And even the solemn, however excellent in sentiment it may be, takes a queer glint in such a sentence—thus emphasized—as 'Would you kindly do *no* sketches, or photos, for *me*, on a Sunday?' The editor of *The Rectory Umbrella* in fact had an inadequate share in either volume of *Sylvie and Bruno*, at which Dodgson laboured, he said, for 'seven or eight hours a day'.

Lewis Carroll was also a very heedful crafts-
man, but even if he had insisted on spelling *can't*
with two apostrophes and *traveller* with one 'l', he
would not have rather petulantly pointed this out,
nor would he have tabulated page by page the
'psychical states' of his characters or given a list of
the scraps of talk he had borrowed for his story
from real little girls and boys. 'Theories' concerning the transference of one's 'immaterial essence'
may be engrossing in the proper place, but that is
not a preface to a fairy-tale.

Nor perhaps would he have set his elfin Sylvie
straying over the sandy themes of 'Drink', teeto-
talism, matrimony, epidemics, cheating at croquet,
conduct in church, Sunday observance and dinner-
party talk. A cautious interest in such matters befits
a sober citizen. But while the insertion of little es-
says on these themes in a nursery book may have
been characteristic of the retiring don—who was
so little known to the public in his later years
that a 'special correspondent' in Oxford spelt his
name *Dogson* throughout an obituary article which
appeared in a leading London newspaper—it was
not characteristic of the Dodgson who when a fond
Victorian mamma invited him to admire a not
easily admirable infant would exclaim with well-
feigned rapture, 'He *is* a baby!'

Not that *Sylvie and Bruno* was intended merely as new lamps for old. The author definitely excused himself from attempting the 'old style' again, not for the sufficing reason that self-imitation is usually disastrous, but because 'all the wayside flowers of Wonderland' had long ago 'been trampled into the dust by others'. He does not seem to have realized that it was *his* clarion alone 'o'er the dreaming earth' that could have raised them from that dust. He apologizes too for mingling grave thoughts on human life with what he hopes will be 'acceptable nonsense'. Acceptable! It is the mingling that is hazardous. Grave thoughts may be wholly at their ease in pages devoted to Nonsense if only they share its medium; and even the solemn is palatable at a Mad Hatter's tea-party when it has the flavour of its austere bread-and-butter. 'If you knew Time as well as I do,' said the Mad Hatter, 'you wouldn't talk about wasting *it*. It's *him*'; ' . . . The rule is jam to-morrow and jam yesterday—but never jam to-day. . .'; 'What does it matter where my body happens to be? My mind goes on working all the same':—haven't such little remarks as these a rather compelling *inward* ring?[1]

[1]Positively to trace, however, the fine degrees by which *sense* progresses towards either of its two extremes, Wisdom and Nonsense, would be a task of the utmost difficulty and

But the White Knight is not the only character in the *Alices* whom one notices looking pensive. 'Never imagine yourself not to be otherwise than what it might appear to others that what you were or might have been was not otherwise than what you had been would have appeared to them to be otherwise.' Or, as Polonius preferred to put it, 'To

---

delicacy. Where shall we look for an analogy? Possibly in the region of Pure Mathematics? This and the mood of the mind that is at home in it may resemble and even neighbour the region and mood of pure Nonsense. The sun that was shining in the middle of the night on the sea and the Walrus and the Carpenter and the oysters may at any rate also have beamed with its own seraphic radiance into the mind of the small boy who made the following attempt to define a vacuum:

'A vacuum is nothing shut up in a box. They have a way of pumping out the air. When all the air and everything else is shut out, naturally they are able to shut in nothing, where the air was before.'

And again:

'A circle is a line of no depth running round a dot for ever.'

Such ventures as these are known as *Howlers*, and have been taken from the mirthful book of that title by Mr. H. Cecil Hunt. Nevertheless they have the vivid limpidity of Nonsense itself. Indeed, with

'Infinity is a place where no one can get to but all lines meet,'

are we not veering into the azure of pure poetry? While as

thine own self be true. . .'. 'In *this* Style 10/6', perhaps; yet if in general Polonius had kept to the other kind of counsel he might also have kept not merely on the safe but on the right side of the arras.

But apart from all 'grave thoughts', the lovely harmonics of any page of the earlier books are

---

for 'Ice = Water that went to sleep in the cold', that comes straight from where Ariel sings a dirge over the relics of him of whose bones coral was made. There is indeed more pure poetry in Carroll's 'You are old, Father William' than there is even of pure prose in Southey's *The Old Man's Comforts*, though in the cantering anapaests of the last two lines in the following stanza Southey almost attains the true *Nirvana*:

'You are old, Father William,' the young man cried,
　'And life must be hastening away;
You are cheerful, and love to converse upon death,
　Now tell me the reason I pray.'

Here, there is no need to await 'the reason', since it is implicit in the verbal *picture*—sober in intention however much otherwise in effect. Its moon-faced 'young man' indeed has come straight out of Lear. And yet Southey was the author of that nursery classic *The Three Bears*!

A poem of Mr. F. W. Harvey's in *September* tells of two small children who having found a dead robin in their garden gave it gentle burial—scattering their flowers over the mound they had raised to remember it by. As they turned again to play, one of them remarked earnestly to the other, 'I *hope* he will have a *happy* dead life.' That too perhaps was Nonsense, but of such is the kingdom of heaven.

only occasionally audible in *Sylvie and Bruno*. *Their* gravity is in as supreme a solution as are the sun and rain and light and chemicals of the soil in a vintage Burgundy. When, too, the mind is at peace in that rare and serene state we call serious—which is as little like the mock solemn or even mere composure as the fool in *Twelfth Night* is like a bore at a dinner-party—it is safe from folly. So also with true Nonsense.

There are memorable gleams and glimmers of the old true magic in these later books; but they are few. Yet, when the first *Sylvie and Bruno* was written, Dodgson was not so old as Defoe when he began *Robinson Crusoe*, and that also has moral intentions. And Serge Aksakov was in his middle sixties when he wrote perhaps the truest, as it is certainly the fullest, of all records of childhood. Whatever the explanation may be, some time after 1871, when *Alice through the Looking-Glass* was published, Lewis Carroll's visits to his old friend unquestionably became fewer. *The Hunting of the Snark*, of 1876, is in the old vein. But even at that, it is not all pure Carroll. And here the flaw is the combining of a nonsense which may to some minds seem a little *too* nonsensical with references which, while nonsensical, are not completely assimilated. The pearl of the *Alices'* oyster reposes in the

Snark's shell, but there are also traces of its primal grit:

> But oh, beamish nephew, beware of the day,
> If your Snark be a Boojum! For then
> You will softly and suddenly vanish away,
> And never be met with again!

There gleams the orient pearl. But this?—

> You may seek it with thimbles—and seek it with care;
> You may hunt it with forks and hope;
> You may threaten its life with a railway-share;
> You may charm it with smiles and soap—. . . .

here, surely, apart from the less delectable melody and rhythm, foreign matter is present; whereas in *Alice* even Father William's little sally on his wife's jaw-bone, even talk in a railway train (with Disraeli in a cocked hat in one corner and a gnat for fretful counsellor) shimmers on with the rest. Not that the first draft even of *Alice* itself was all pure *Alice* as we know it now, for it contained a chapter about Wasps which, on the candid and un-solicited advice of Tenniel, Carroll afterwards decided to omit.

These are, of course, critical needle-points, and of no less delicate an issue, in relation to their con-text, than the attempt to compare the poetical merits, in *their* context, of 'O what can ail thee, knight-at-arms . . . ?' and of 'Ah, what can ail

C 33

thee, wretched wight . . . ?'; an issue more delicate yet when we have to choose between 'Many a summer's suns have shone' and 'Many a summer's sun has shone'; but easier again when our choice lies between,

> With never a whisper on the main
> Off shot the spectre ship,

and

> With far-heard whisper o'er the sea
> Off shot the spectre-bark.

So with any question of humour, and therefore of Nonsense. What species of invisibility is comparable to that of the joke un-seen? Coventry Patmore, for example, once told Dodgson that Wordsworth on some occasion assured his friends that, so far as he was aware, he had been personally responsible for only one joke in his complete mortal existence. Out one morning on a solitary and inspiring walk he met a carter who stopped him and enquired if he had seen his—the carter's—wife. 'My good friend,' said Wordsworth, 'I didn't know you *had* a wife.' . . . Now, not to be able to *see* this joke (as Wordsworth saw it) is nothing of course but a misfortune. And so it may be with the soap in the *Snark*.[1]

[1]'The pleasure of wit', says Dr. Sigmund Freud in his treatise on the subject,

'originates from an *economy of expenditure in inhibition*, of the

But whatever may have happened to Lewis Carroll in these later years, the small boy in Dodgson who had fallen in love at first sight with logarithms, who armed earthworms with tiny sections of clay pipe, and revelled in puns and puzzles,

---

comic from an *economy of expenditure in thought*, and of humour from an *economy of expenditure in feeling*. All three activities of our psychic apparatus derive pleasure from economy. They all strive to bring back from the psychic activity a pleasure which has really been lost in the development of this activity. In the euphoria which we are thus striving to obtain is nothing but the state of a bygone time in which we were wont to defray our psychic work with slight expenditure. It is the state of our childhood, in which we did not know the comic, were incapable of wit, and did not need humour to make us happy.'

Examples might a little enlighten this analysis (and its 'activities'); but what is to be said of its last peculiar statement? The very greenest of nursery goslings, surely, can enjoy the comic; I once knew a small boy of five or so who having properly admired what to his ear had sounded like 'the bolar bear' immediately enquired with much amusement if he might now see the top-hat species; and in *The Sayings of the Children* it is recorded that four-year-old 'Two', having heard his mother order the waggonette, unhesitatingly capped it with, 'I suppose you wag along in the waggonette, the landau lands you at the door, and you sweep off in the brougham'—which is at least on the way to (Shakespearean) wit. And the only reason Marjorie Fleming was never in positive '*need*' of humour seems to have been that she had so copious a supply of it.

lived on. He was his own happiest company in his solitude at Christ Church; and college life, he said, is 'by no means unmixed misery'. There this recluse indulged in more hobbies than the king in the story in the *Arabian Nights* had horses. The foremost of them was being methodical. He first summarized, then filed, all his letters. He kept lists of the unanswered—containing sometimes as many as seventy or eighty names—and to such admirable effect that he once apologized to a friend for not acknowledging a letter twenty-four months old, and sent his thanks to another for a present that had reached him five years before.

He was a skilful amateur photographer ('in the wet process'), his portraiture being remarkable for his original attempts at 'pictorial effects', and he particularly enjoyed practising his art on a distinguished sitter. He invented a system of mnemonics and of electoral reform, a postage-stamp case, poetical acrostics and the nyctograph, and he improved the game of backgammon. He published a volume of parodies, chiefly of Tennyson and even of Longfellow, but none quite equal to 'Will you walk a little faster?' or 'Beautiful Soup'. He wrote a little treatise on Reading. Feed the mind, at intervals, he advised, as you should the body, on a diet not too rich or too miscellaneous, and let it be *consciously* digested. As with Thackeray's bun and the small boy so with a good book and the deserving grown-up: he will devour it at *any* moment—

> O what fun!
> A nice plum bun!
> How I wish
> It never was done!

In *Wise Words about Letter Writing*, again, the author counselled his reader to write clearly and therefore slowly—his own graceful handwriting and ingenious monogram being exemplary; to address the envelope *first*; not to *seem* in earnest when writing in jest; and in the event of a correspondence with a friend becoming a little heated, always to let one's tat for his tit be a shade less severe and a full tone more friendly. And last, he advised, never post an angry letter on the day it is written. Indeed, such is Time's leech-craft that but one night's sweet repose may wholly assuage the sharpest of wounds even to one's Vanity!

Dodgson's own letters, even when intended to be playful, were apt, as I have said, to be a little dry. But though he once played a joke on one of his little girls which was not quite successful, he kept the rules which he himself laid down—rules that are easily elastic enough to welcome the very

far from dry—the inexhaustibly Queery-Leary
epistles, for example, of the author of *There was an
Old Man who said, ' Hush!'*:

> ... So then I hope to hear your ways
> Are bent on English moves
> For that I trust once more to gaze
> Upon the friend I loves. ...
>
> But if you are not coming now
> Just write a line to say so—
> And I shall still consider how
> Ajoskyboskybayso.
>
> No more my pen: no more my ink:
> No more my rhyme is clear.
> So I shall leave off here I think—
> Yours ever,
>
> Edward Lear.

Dodgson was actively interested in public affairs,
too. When the erection of a belfry in Tom Quad
was proposed he made witty sport of the design
—in both senses of the word: 'Its chief architec-
tural merit is its simplicity—a simplicity so pure,
so profound, in a word so *simple* that no other
word will fitly describe it.' If only all right-minded
controversialists would dip their pens into ink as
quiet and as fatal. In *The Dynamics of a Parti-cle*, on
the other hand, the fancy of the mathematician is
at play. This pamphlet appeared in 1865 when Mr.
Gladstone was contesting (in vain) the seat he had

held at Oxford University for eighteen years, and it proved to be not of a kind that appealed to his sense of humour.

Apart from *A Game of Logic* and *A Tangled Tale* with ten stubborn 'knots' in it, Dodgson invented also no less than four parlour paper pastimes, which he called Misch-masch, Doublets, Lanricks and Syzygies, the last so ingeniously elaborated that one aspiring novice spent a large part of a Sabbath morning in the attempt to master merely its rules for scoring.

Mathematics indeed, and her sister science Logic, were not only his serious occupation but the delight of his leisure. He was at times a poor sleeper and to while away the lagging hours and, as he confessed, to keep trespassing thoughts at bay, he set himself 'Pillow Problems', and invented a method of recording them in the dark. Alas, even these, quite apart from his *Euclid and his Modern Rivals*, lie far beyond the scope of this paper, and, that being so, a friend who insists on remaining anony mous has very kindly allowed me to quote his remarks on them :

'These problems were intended', he says, 'for those who possess the necessary intellectual equipment to tackle them and would all probably be classed by mathematicians as "elementary" because their solution does not require the use of the Calculus, but only Arithmetic, Algebra, Geometry and Trigonometry; but this is not to say that they are easy. That would hardly be expected of the author. Many of them are of a somewhat unusual character, and require the use of some ingenious device which would not readily occur to most solvers, even with the aid of paper and pencil. In some cases the construction of the problem[1] is an almost

[1]The following may be quoted as an example:

'Five friends agreed to form themselves into a Wine-Company (Limited). They contributed equal amounts of wine, which had been bought at the same price. They then elected one of themselves to act as Treasurer; and another of them undertook to act as Salesman, and to sell the wine at 10 *per cent.* over cost price.

'The first day the Salesman drank one bottle, sold some, and handed over the receipts to the Treasurer.

'The second day he drank none, but pocketed the profits on one bottle sold, and handed over the rest of the receipts to the Treasurer.

'That night the Treasurer visited the cellars, and counted the remaining wine. "It will fetch just £11," he muttered to himself as he left the cellars.

'The third day the Salesman drank one bottle, pocketed the profits on another, and handed over the rest of the receipts to the Treasurer.

'The wine was now all gone; the Company held a meeting, and found to their chagrin that their profits (*i.e.* the Treasurer's receipts, less the original value of the wine) only cleared 6*d.* a bottle of the whole stock. These profits had

more remarkable performance than its solution, for the author must have foreseen the details as well as the method of their working, otherwise he would not have been able to arrange his figures so that the answers "come out".

'Whimsical touches appear occasionally; two of the problems, for example, postulate the existence of a triangular billiard-table. A few are put into the form of a tale; and sometimes an essential element of the problem is concealed in a casual and apparently unimportant reference.

'The author had a fondness, also, for the problem of probabilities, and the most startling example of this is the following: "A bag contains two counters, of which nothing is known except that each is either white or black. Ascertain their col-

---

accrued in 3 equal sums on the three days (*i.e.* the Treasurer's receipts for the day, less the original value of the wine taken out during the day, had come to the same amount every time); but of course only the Salesman knew this.

'(1) How much wine had they bought? (2) At what price?'

In this problem the *number* of friends would seem at first sight to be immaterial; but this is not the case. The answer to the problem as proposed is that 60 bottles were bought at 8*s*. 4*d*. each; but if there had been *four* friends in the Company instead of *five* the answer to the same problem would have been 48 bottles at 10*s*. each.

ours without taking them out of the bag." ' The author proved—to his own satisfaction at least—that one of the counters must have been white and the other black. In most minds, however, such a puzzle will produce nothing more than a small, if charming, vacuum. It reminds me—though, why, I cannot say—of the only ball Dodgson ever bowled in a cricket match. It would have been a wide, he said, if it had reached the wicket.

Compared with any such problem, at any rate, a passing reference like 'The Apodoses of these two Hypotheticals are incompatible,' in a playful little puzzle concerning Uncle Jim and Uncle Joe and their three barbers, is but child's-play. We merely fly to a dictionary. But there must be many devotees of Lewis Carroll who would find themselves faltering in the presence of the mathematical don.

The well-known story, none the less, that Queen Victoria, captivated by *Alice in Wonderland*, sent for the rest of its author's works, and was thereupon presented (by his publisher) with copies of *The Condensation of Determinants*, and *A Syllabus of Plane Algebraical Geometry*, is too good to be true. It was denied by Dodgson himself in *Symbolic Logic*. But there is another little story of Queen Victoria and Alice, both of them supreme characters in their several spheres, which is true beyond question. And it is a pleasure and privilege to be permitted by the friend who shared in it, but who, alas, withholds her name, to record it here.

When she was a little girl of three and a half, before she could read, that is, though not before she could be read to, she was sitting one winter's afternoon on a footstool by the fireside looking at the pictures in *Wonderland*, while a favourite and favoured aunt conversed with the Queen and her ladies at the adjacent tea-table. Noticing presently this rapt doubled-up little creature in the fire-light so intent over her book, the Queen asked her what it was. She rose and carried it over, and standing at the royal knee opened it at the page where tinied Alice is swimming in the flood of her own tears. Five years had gone by since the Prince Consort's death, but the Queen was still attired in widow's weeds, in solemn black. Putting two and two together (as only Dodgson with the help of Carroll could), this little girl, pointing at the picture, looked up into the Queen's face, and said: 'Do you think, please, *you* could cry as much as that?'

The profound hush that followed while the ladies in the room pondered this bold enquiry was broken by the Queen's reply—which, now, I fear

—though it was so ardent a tribute to Carroll that even Dodgson might have welcomed it—is no longer recoverable. Next day, however, a tiny locket, with a design of intertwined horse-shoes in coral and seed pearls and with a minute portrait of the widowed Queen within, and this packed in a charming little box with the royal monogram on the lid, was despatched from Windsor by a special messenger in a most resplendent uniform. It remains a precious souvenir of those few tense moments.

The point of this little incident, if anything so childlike and tender can be said to have anything so sharp, is that the author of a book as remote from the realm of phantasy as *Leaves from a Journal of our Life in the Highlands* could share her delight in *Wonderland* with one of the youngest of her subjects. But that is precisely its supreme achievement. It is, in the words[1] of Sir Walter Besant, one of the very few books in the world 'which can be read with equal pleasure by old and young. . . . It is the only child's book of nonsense that is never

[1]These I have taken from a letter to a friend, Mrs. Herbert Fuller, herself one of Lewis Carroll's little girls and also the mother of one whose happy thought it was to endow a cot in the Children's Hospital, Great Ormond Street, to his memory.

childish.' And not only that; it admits us into a state of being which, until it was written, was not only unexplored but undiscovered. Nevertheless like other rare achievements it was the fruit apparently of a happy accident. For once in a while the time and the place and the loved one came together.

On the afternoon of 4 July 1862, in the Long Vacation, a minute expedition set out from Oxford up the river to Godstow. It returned laden with a treasure compared with which that of the *Golden Hind* was but dross. It consisted of Canon Duckworth, then a tutor at Christ Church and the 'duck' in the story itself, of Dodgson, and the three little Liddells, whom Dodgson had nicknamed Prima, Secunda and Tertia. They were, each in her own degree, members of a happy band of children who were the delight and solace of Carroll's long years at Christ Church. A few of them remained his intimate friends. But in general they reigned in turn as briefly as the Aprils that have followed one another throughout the centuries. He collected them wherever he had the good fortune to find them, especially, so it seems, at the seaside and in railway trains. It is related that, bound for the beach, he would leave his lodgings at Eastbourne armed not only with puzzles but with a supply of large safety pins, in case any little girl intent on paddling should be in need of one. Unlike most other dons, he provided not cakes or lollipops for their entertainment in his 'large, lofty and extremely cheerful-looking study', where he insisted on keeping all his furniture and carpets in precise alignment, but a musical box, toys and an old Woolly Bear, not to mention home-made devices for lighting his gas and for boiling his kettle. In London he took them to plays and pantomimes, and blessed any small actresses who shone behind the footlights with a like generosity and kindness. However brief the reign of these (occasionally fractious) little princesses, he was faithfully fickle to one and all of them—each in turn. Not so with small boys. Bruno is a compound of imp, elf and infant Samuel, and hardly therefore an exception. But for small boys in real life Dodgson and even Carroll professed an aversion 'almost amounting to terror'. But then, as Mrs. Meynell has pointed out, small boys in Art have never been neglected. It was Carroll's prerogative 'to make great amends to little girls'.

Of the three children who accompanied him to Godstow that afternoon, it was Secunda—Alice Pleasance Liddell—'courteous, trustful, wildly curious . . . loving as a dog and gentle as a fawn',

46

—and of a wistful childlike loveliness that would have been the delight of Leonardo—who was destined as 'Alice' to be immortal. She was the mistress jewel in his carcanet. They paddled on; Duckworth was stroke of the 'pair', Dodgson bow, and *Alice's Adventures Underground* were told, on and on, over stroke's shoulder to Secunda who, with her sisters, and ropes in lap, sat at the tiller. 'Yes,' the skipper agreed, on the question being put to him, 'I am inventing as we go along.' Carroll was then thirty, Blake being two years older when his *Songs of Innocence* were published. And though a moment's reflection might have prepared us for this, off-hand these ages are surprising. Why does one far rather expect say, *sixty* and *sixty*-two?

Now afternoons in July, if fair and cloudless, are apt to be narcotic. The rhythm of sculling quiets the mind and sets the workaday wits drowsing. The low secret chuckle of the water, the lovely light on its surface, rimpling up into those three rapt little faces, would have decoyed any imagination into activity. And Carroll's voice flowed gently on to the accompaniment of the whispering of the river, the dipping swallows and the faint stir of the wind in the branches at the water-side.

It was at Duckworth's suggestion that he laboured on into the small hours that evening, pen and paper for company, and midnight oil for illumination. 'His memory was so good', said his friend, 'that I think the story as he wrote it down was almost word by word the same as he had told it in the boat.' The manuscript was bestowed on the Deanery, and here Henry Kingsley chanced on it. Why should such a treasure remain hidden under a bushel? He urged Mrs. Liddell to persuade its author to publish it, and suggested Tenniel as illustrator. *Alice's Hour in Elfland* having been discarded as a title, it appeared exactly three years afterwards, and in spite of its temporary withdrawal from circulation owing to the poor reproduction of its pictures, it instantly enchanted those dreadfully matter-of-fact Victorians and has never since suffered the faintest eclipse.

Of few masterpieces have we so particularized a birthday. 'Up the river', ran Carroll's Journal for 4 July, and then, 'I told them the fairy tale.' 'Alice' herself, moreover, has not only recorded her belief that the story was begun one summer afternoon 'when the sun was so burning hot' that the little party took refuge in a meadow down the river in 'the only bit of shade to be found under a new-made hay-rick', but she has also explained that she herself persuaded Carroll to write it down.

Dr. Paget, on the other hand, could recall a mathematical Reading Party at Whitby as far back as the summer of 1854, when the story, he said, was 'incubated' by Dodgson, then only twenty-two, to amuse a circle of eager youngsters of both sexes:

> 'Twas there he rested on a rock
> Conveniently low:
> And all the little Oysters stood
> And waited in a row.

Yet another version is that Carroll wrote *Wonderland* to amuse and comfort a remote little relative of his when she was ill. And the moral of *that* is, it couldn't be so; since only one paragraph of such a panacea would have sufficed to make her quite better.

And last, while the *Life* records that it was George MacDonald who persuaded Carroll to publish his story, yet another account avers it was the wild applause of six-year-old little Greville MacDonald, to whom with his sisters Carroll read *Wonderland* from its manuscript, that had this effect. As for the weather, *The Times* of 5 July 1862 maintains that the previous day was occasionally rainy, and its temperature only 53°.

These varying accounts, however, are no doubt easily reconcilable and, like Homer's many birthplaces, they are a telling tribute to the poet who was the adequate cause of them.

What they have in common is evidence that the tale, rhymes and all, and 'finished' to the finest edge of craftsmanship, seems for the most part to have floated into Carroll's mind as spontaneously as did one of the best known lines in English verse: 'For the Snark was a Boojum, you see.' 'Every word of the dialogue', he said, 'came of itself.' And though he confesses elsewhere that his 'jaded muse was' at times 'goaded into action . . . more because she had to say something than because she had something to say'; and that he despatched Alice down the rabbit-hole not knowing in the least what was to become of her; and though, whenever the crystal wellspring ceased to flow, he could always pretend to fall fast asleep (whereas of course he had actually come wide-awake)—all this little affects the marvel, and is interesting mainly because Dodgson in *Sylvie and Bruno* expressed his contempt for any writing that was chiefly the result of taking pains. He maintained that all such writing cannot but remain unimpassioned and uninspired.

What, then, of the scorned delights, and the laborious days; what of the loading of every rift with ore; and that midnight oil in the study of Christ Church? Were these the sighs of a Dodgson weeping over a lost Carroll? Or was it merely that, with advancing age, he himself, like most elderly writers, when recalling the light that shone upon their youthful achievements and the dews that dropped on them from heaven, forgot the care, the patience and the pains? Yet another marvel is that *Wonderland* should have been followed by so consummate a sequel as *Through the Looking-Glass.* They are twin stars on whose *relative* radiance alone literary astronomers may be left to disagree.

Both stories have a structural framework—in the one playing-cards, in the other a game of chess, the moves in which Dodgson only to some extent attempted to justify. These no doubt suggested a few of his chief characters, or rather their social status; but what other tale-teller could have made Carroll's use of them? All that he owed to the device of the looking-glass, except that it is one which has perplexed and delighted child, philosopher and savage alike, is that the handwriting in the story is the wrong way round, and that when Alice wished to go forwards she had to walk backwards—a method of progression that is sometimes of service even in life itself. Both stories, too —and this is a more questionable contrivance, particularly as it introduces a rather sententious elder sister—turn out to be dreams; and one little girl I know of burst out crying when the final awakening came.

All this however affects the imaginative reality —the supreme illusion—of the *Alices* no more than its intricate chronology and knowledge of the law affect that of *Wuthering Heights*, and these have been proved to be unassailable. In reading the Carroll stories, that is, we scarcely notice, however consistent and admirable it may be, their ingenious design. And that is true also of *As You Like It*. Quite apart from any such design, at any rate, they would still remain in essence perhaps the most *original* books in the world. Indeed the genius in Carroll seems to have worked more subtly than the mind which it was possessed by realized. It is a habit genius has.

Then again, the Queen of Hearts, he said himself, was intended to be 'a blind and aimless Fury', the Red Queen was to reveal 'the concentrated essence of all governesses', the Mad Hatter was once a don, the White Queen strongly reminded him of Mrs. Wragge in Wilkie Collins's *No Name*, and the White Knight was intended to characterize the speaker in Wordsworth's *Resolution and Independence*. But if he had been merely as successful as *that*, where would these immortals be now? The reason is in service to the imagination, not *vice versa.* 'Please never *praise* me at all,' Dodgson entreated a child who had written to him about the *Alices.* 'I just feel myself a trustee, that is all.' So might Nature herself reply if one commended her for the inexhaustible versatility of design revealed in her hippopotamus, her camel, her angel-fishes and her flea!

So too with the *Snark.* 'I am very much afraid', wrote Dodgson, 'I didn't mean anything but nonsense. . . . But since words mean more than we mean to express when we use them . . . whatever good meanings are in the book I am very glad to accept as the meaning of the book'—a remark which is not only modest and generous but well worth pondering.

The intellectual thread, none the less, which runs through the *Alices* is the reverse of being negligible. It is on this that their translucent beads of phantasy are strung, and it is the more effective for being so consistent and artfully concealed. As in the actual writing of poetry the critical faculties of the poet are in a supreme and constant activity, so with the *Alices.* Their 'characters', for example, in all their rich diversity are in exquisite keeping with one another. It may too have been due not to design but to happy accident (a remark that applies to Lear's limericks but not to most books aimed at the young, however wide they may fall of the mark) that though both books were written for children, the only child in them, apart from an occasional infant, is Alice herself. The Mad Hatter is perennial forty, the Carpenter is of the age of all carpenters, the Red King is, say, the age Henry VIII was born, while the Queens and the Duchess —well, they know best about that.

Alice herself, of course, with her familiar little toss of the head, with her serene mobile face, courteous, amiable, except when she *must* speak up for herself, easily reconciled, inclined to tears, but tears how swiftly dashed away; with her dignity, her matter-of-factness, her conscientiousness, her courage (even in the most outlandish of circumstances) never to submit or yield; and with one of the most useful of all social resources, the art of changing a conversation—what a tribute she is not only to her author but to Victorian childhood! Capable, modest, demure, sedate, they are words a little out of fashion nowadays; but Alice alone would redeem them all. And even if now and then she is a trifle superior, a trifle *too* demure, must not even the most delicate of simple and arduous little samplers have its wrong side?

She might indeed have been a miniature model of all the Victorian virtues and still have fallen short if it were not for her freedom from silliness and her saving good sense—a good sense that never bespangles itself by becoming merely clever. However tart and touchy, however queer and querulous and quarrelsome her 'retinue' in Wonderland and in Looking-Glass Land may be, and she all but always gets the worst of every argument, it is this sagacity of mind and heart that keeps her talk from being merely 'childish' and theirs from seeming grown-uppish, and, in one word, prevents the hazardous situation from falling into the non-nonsensical. She wends serenely on like a quiet moon in a chequered sky. Apart, too, from an occasional Carrollian comment, the sole medium of the stories is *her* pellucid consciousness: an ideal preached by Henry James himself, and practised—in how different a setting—in *What Maisie Knew*.

It is this rational poise in a topsy-turvy world (a world seen upside-down, as M. Cammaerts says, and looking far more healthy and bright) that gives the two tales their exquisite balance. For though laws there certainly are in the realm of Nonsense, they are all of them unwritten laws. Its subjects obey them unaware of any restrictions. Anything may happen there except only what can't happen *there*. Its kings and queens are kings and queens for precisely the same reason that the Mock Turtle is a Mock Turtle, even though once he was a real Turtle—by a divine right, that is, on which there is no need to insist. A man there, whether he be Tweedledum or the Carpenter or the White Knight, apart from his being a gentleman so perfect that you do not notice it, is never 'a man for a' that', simply because there isn't any 'a' that'. And though 'morals' pepper their pages—'Everything's got a moral if only you can find it'—the stories themselves have none. 'In fact', as Carroll said himself, 'they do not teach anything at all'.

Instead, they stealthily instil into us a unique state of mind. Their jam—wild strawberry—*is* the powder—virgin gold-dust—though we may never be conscious of its cathartic effects. Although, too, Carroll's Nonsense in itself, in Dryden's words, may be such that it 'never can be understood',there is no need to understand it. It is self-evident: and indeed may vanish away if we try to do so. Precisely the converse is true of the sober-sided order of nonsense. The longer we ponder on that the more hollowly the tub resounds, the drabber grows the day. The *Alices* lighten our beings like sunshine, like that divine rainbow in the skies beneath which the living things of the world went out into radiance and freedom from the narrow darkness of the Ark. And any mind in their influence is freed the while from all its cares. Carroll's Wonderland indeed is a (queer little) universe of the mind resembling Einstein's in that it is a finite infinity endlessly explorable though never to be explored. How blue are its heavens, how grass-green its grass—its fauna and flora being more curiously reviving company not only than any but the pick of *this* world's but than those of almost any other book I know. And even for variety and precision, from the Mad Hatter down to Bill the Lizard, that company is rivalled only by the novelists who are as generous as they are skilled—an astonishing feat, since Carroll's creations are not only of his own species but of his own genus.

Just, too, as in the talk in the *Alices* we realize the meaning of a remark made by a writer in the old *Spectator*: 'Nothing is capable of being well set to music that is not nonsense,' contrariwise, to invert a reference to the law in *The Antiquary*, what sounds like flawless sense in them may be flawless *non*sense for all that. '*Must* a name mean something?' was Alice's first question to Humpty Dumpty. 'Of course it must,' said Humpty Dumpty with a short laugh. '*My* name means the shape I am. . . . With a name like yours, you might be any shape, almost.'

Whose is the nonsense here, Humpty Dumpty's or the London Directory's—where Smiths may be grocers, Coopers haberdashers, and Bakers butchers? And what (on earth) would any man look like if he looked like a Wilkinson, a Marjoribanks or a John James Jones? Charles Dickens alone could say. Then again Humpty Dumpty's 'Let's go back to the last remark but one' (an unfailing resource in any heated argument), his 'If I'd meant that, I'd have said it,' his '*One* can't, perhaps, but *two* can,' and his righteous indignation with a person who doesn't know a cravat from a belt—well, not even a Lord Chief Justice in a black cap could be more incisive and more to the rational point.

What, too, even from a strictly conventional point of view, is unusual, unpractical, amiss in the Duchess's kitchen? She is gracing it with her presence, and these are democratic times; she is nursing her baby, and *noblesse oblige*; and the kitchen is full of smoke, which Victorian kitchens often were. What do we expect in a kitchen? A cook, a fire, a cat, and a cauldron with soup in it. It is precisely what we get—and, to give it flavour, someone has been a little free with the pepper. The cook, it is true, is throwing frying-pans and saucepans at her mistress, but nowadays there's many a lady in the land who would forgive the fusillade if only she

could secure the cook. As for the Duchess's remarks, they are as appropriate as they are peremp-
tory. And do we not expect the high-born to be a
little high-handed? Alice enquires why her cat
grins like that.

'It's a Cheshire cat,' she says, 'and that's why.'

Alice smiled that she didn't know cats *could* grin.

'They all can,' said the Duchess, 'and most of
them do.'

Alice didn't know of any that did.

'You don't know much,' said the Duchess, 'and
that's a fact.'

She goes on to remark that the world would be
much improved if everybody in it minded his own
business; and the only defect in that little grumble
is that it is a counsel of perfection. Surely too when
cosmological explanations of 'how the earth ro-
tates on its axis' are about, one's sole resource is to
chop off somebody's head.

As for the lullaby the Duchess sings as she sits
—long-coated, broad-grinned infant in lap—in
that marvellous head-dress, square knees apart,
dour and indomitable, it preaches justice in the
first stanza and proves her personal practice of it
in the last:

> Speak roughly to your little boy,
> And beat him when he sneezes:

>He only does it to annoy,
>   Because he knows it teases.
>   *Wow! wow! wow!*
>
>I speak severely to my boy,
>   I beat him when he sneezes;
>For he can thoroughly enjoy
>   The pepper when he pleases!
>   *Wow! wow! wow!*

Such discipline—those nursery *wows*—may sound a little harsh in the kindergartens of our own baby-ridden age, but it was on this basis Victorian mothers brought up the pioneers of our Empire!

So far, so practical. But it must not be forgotten that this 'large kitchen' into which nine-inch Alice had so unceremoniously intruded belonged to a little house in a wood only about four feet high, nor that the Duchess's grunting infant as soon as it breathes the open air in Alice's arms turns placidly into a small pig. And that, except metaphorically, children don't do. Not in real life, that is. Only in *dreams*.

And it is here that we stumble on *the* sovereign element in the *Alices*. It consists in the presentation of what is often perfectly rational, practical, logical, and, maybe, mathematical, what is terse, abrupt and pointed, in a state and under conditions of life to which we most of us win admittance only when we are blessedly asleep. To every man his own dreams, to every man his own day-dreams. And as with sense, nonsense and un-sense; as with me, you and a sort of us-ishness; as with past, future and the all-and-almost-nothing in between; so with Greenwich time, time and *dream* time; with good motives, bad motives, and dream motives; self, better self and dream self. Dreaming is another state of being, with laws as stringent *and* as elastic as those of the world of Nonsense. And what dream in literature has more blissfully refreshed a prose-ridden world than the dream which gently welled into Dodgson's mind that summer afternoon, nearly seventy years ago, when, sculls in hand and eyes fixed on little Alice Liddell's round-orbed countenance, the Lewis Carroll in him slipped off into Wonderland?

Who can say what influences one silent consciousness may have upon another? May it not be to some magical suffusion and blending of these two, the mathematician's and the child's, that we owe the *Alices*? Even the technical triumph of the two books consists in having made what is finally declared to be a dream actually and always *seem* to be a dream. Open either of them at random; ask yourself any one of the questions on the page exposed; endeavour to find an answer not merely as apt and pungent as are most answers of the *Alice* order, but one that will at the same time fret by not so much as a hair's breadth the story's dream-like crystalline tissue: and then turn back to the book for *Carroll's* answer. That alone, though a trivial one, will be proof enough of the quality of his genius.

And what of the visionary light, the colour, the scenery; that wonderful seascape, for example, in *The Walrus and the Carpenter*, as wide as Milton's in *Il Penseroso*—the quality of its sea, its sands, its space and distances? What of the exquisite transition from one setting on to another in a serene seductive discontinuity in—for but one example—the chapter entitled 'Wool and Water'? First the little dark shop and the hunched-up placid old sheep, with her forest of knitting-needles, who but an instant before was the White Queen; then the cumbrous gliding boat on that queer glutinous water, among the scented rushes—'dream rushes' that melt away 'almost like snow' in Alice's lap; and then, without the faintest jar, back into the little dark shop again—Platonic original of all little dark shops. All this is of the world of dreams and of that world alone. The *Alices* indeed have the timelessness, the placelessness, and an atmosphere resembling in their own odd fashion not only those of the *Songs of Innocence* and Traherne's

Meditations, but of the medieval descriptions of paradise and many of the gem-like Italian pictures of the fifteenth century. This atmosphere is conveyed, as it could alone be conveyed, in a prose of limpid simplicity, as frictionless as the unfolding of the petals of an evening primrose in the cool of twilight; a prose, too, that could be the work only of a writer who like John Ruskin had from his earliest years examined every word he used with a scrupulous attention:—

'It succeeded beautifully. She had not been walking a minute before she found herself face to face with the Red Queen, and full in sight of the hill she had been so long aiming at.

' "Where do you come from?" said the Red Queen. "And where are you going? Look up, speak nicely, and don't twiddle your fingers all the time."

'Alice attended to all these directions, and explained, as well as she could, that she had lost her way.

' "I don't know what you mean by *your* way," said the Queen: "all the ways about here belong to *me*—but why did you come out here at all?" she added in a kinder tone. "Curtsey while you're thinking what to say. It saves time."

'Alice wondered a little at this, but she was too

much in awe of the Queen to disbelieve it. "I'll try it when I go home," she thought to herself, "the next time I'm a little late for dinner."

' "It's time for you to answer now," the Queen said, looking at her watch: "open your mouth a *little* wider when you speak, and always say 'your Majesty.' "

' "I only wanted to see what the garden was like, your Majesty——"

' "That's right," said the Queen, patting her on the head, which Alice didn't like at all: "though, when you say 'garden,' *I've* seen gardens, compared with which this would be a wilderness."

'Alice didn't dare to argue the point, but went on: "——and I thought I'd try and find my way to the top of that hill——"

' "When you say 'hill', " the Queen interrupted, "*I* could show you hills, in comparison with which you'd call that a valley."

' "No, I shouldn't," said Alice, surprised into contradicting her at last: "a hill *ca'n't* be a valley, you know. That would be nonsense——"

'The Red Queen shook her head. "You may call it 'nonsense' if you like," she said, "but *I've* heard nonsense, compared with which that would be as sensible as a dictionary!"

'Alice curtseyed again, as she was afraid from

the Queen's tone that she was a *little* offended: and they walked on in silence till they got to the top of the little hill.

'For some minutes Alice stood without speaking, looking out in all directions over the country —and a most curious country it was. . . .'

A most curious country it *is*—how silent, how solitary, how remote—and yet one incomparably less so than that is the memory and imagination of this strange meditative queen all of whose 'ways' beyond any manner of question *belong* to *her*! What relation any such region of the world of dreams has to the world of our actual, who can say? Our modern oneiromantics have their science, but the lover of the *Alices* is in no need of it. What relation any such dream-world has to some other state of being seen only in glimpses here and now might be a more valuable but is an even less answerable question. In any case, and even though there are other delights in them which only many years' experience of life can fully reveal, it is the child that is left in us who tastes the sweetest honey and laves its imagination in the clearest waters to be found in the *Alices*.

How the books fare in translation—in Hebrew, in Chinese, in Irish, for example—I am, alas, unable to say. Since however their species of nonsense is purely their own, we must not too complacently flatter ourselves that it is also wholly English, quite apart from its being how oddly verdant an oasis amid what we are pleased to contemn as such quantities of Victorian sand. To be too solemn about it, to turn these tiny classics into an intelligence test and their Alice into an examination paper, would, as Mr. Chesterton has warned us, be little short of a miracle of Georgian stupidity. Any such perils defied, may that nonsense in all its varieties continue to blossom like the almond tree: the oaks of the forest will flourish none the less bravely in its floral company. Indeed there are times and crises in affairs not only personal, but public, political and even international, when the following tribute from M. Cammaerts may first serve for a solace and then for a solemn warning:—

'The English', he says, 'speak, in an off-hand way, of "possessing a Sense of Humour" or of not possessing it, little realising that this sense, with the meaning they attach to it, is almost unique in the world, and can be acquired only after years of strenuous and patient effort. For many foreigners, Einstein's theories present fewer difficulties than certain limericks. . . .'

Than certain limericks! We can at need, that is, while still we keep the mint, dole out these pre-

cious coppers whensoever the too, too intellectual
alien proves intractable, while for our own precious island currency we can treasure the gold of
the crystal-watered land of Havilah—Carroll's and
the *Alices*'. And if at any time in the solitude of
our hearts we ourselves need an unfaltering and
unflattering critic, which is not unseldom, there
is always the Cheshire Cat.